AL

—1

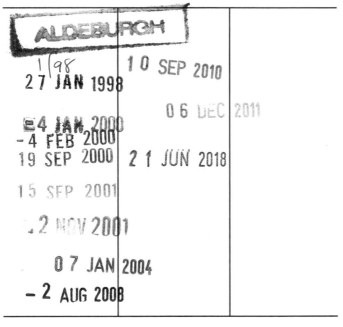

Suffolk County Council
Libraries & Heritage

AL

You may keep this item until the last date stamped below.
Providing it has not been reserved by another customer, you may renew it, either by visiting any Suffolk library, or by post-quoting the item's barcode number, your library card number, name, address and telephone number. Unfortunately, items cannot be renewed by telephone.

ALDEBURGH

1/98
27 JAN 1998

10 SEP 2010

06 DEC 2011

24 JAN 2000
-4 FEB 2000
19 SEP 2000

21 JUN 2018

15 SEP 2001

2 NOV 2001

07 JAN 2004

-2 AUG 2008

Any overdue charges on this item will be made at the current ADULT rate.

942.610

Norfolk Museums Service

Sue Margeson PhD FSA, 1948-1997
Sue, as Keeper of Archaeology at Norwich Castle Museum,
completed this book during her last illness

© Norfolk Museums Service 1997

ISBN 0 903101 65 3

Designed by NPS - Graphic Design:
Kevin Matthews

Illustrations by Steven Ashley, Trevor Ashwin, Anne Holness,
Kenneth Penn, Hoste Spalding, Susan White

Photographs of objects by David Wicks

First published 1997

Front cover: Norfolk objects, see p.28 photo by David Wicks

Acknowledgments
I should like to thank James Graham-Campbell, Kevin Leahy, Caroline Richardson,
John Newman, and Sue Youngs for their invaluable help in discussing the metalwork. I
am also very grateful to the metal-detector users who have made Viking artefacts available
for study at the Castle Museum, Norwich.

I should also like to thank Susie West for all her assistance in preparing
the manuscript and seeing the book through the press.

The Landscape Archaeology Section and the Norfolk Archaeological Unit provided assistance with the preparation of figures and plates especially for this book.

CONTENTS

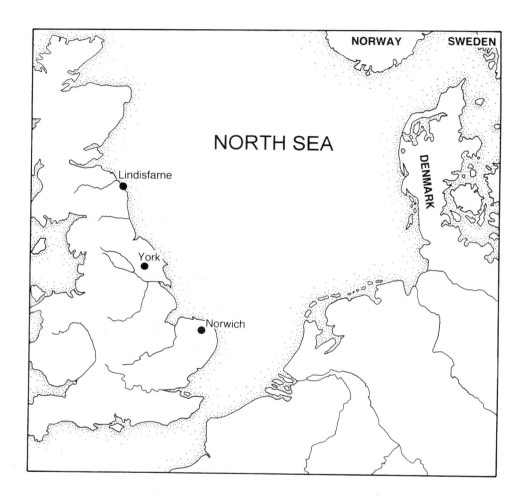

NORWAY   SWEDEN

NORTH SEA

DENMARK

Lindisfarne

York

Norwich

Fig 1. Location map of Viking homelands and Britain
MAP BY TREVOR ASHWIN
(All figures copyright Norfolk Museums Service unless otherwise stated)

The MAKING
of the DANELAW

The Vikings who swept across northern Europe in sleek warships have always caught the imagination, for their daring exploits and sheer bravado. The word 'Viking' literally means one who fights at sea. Invasions, battles, looting and pillaging are still in popular imagination the hallmarks of the Vikings. Yet their achievements at home in Norway, Sweden and Denmark, and in establishing colonies and settlements in far-flung corners of the world are no less astonishing. For three centuries, from the 8th to the 11th, the Vikings flourished. Their engineering capabilities in designing ships, in building causeways and fortresses are impressive, and their trading exploits across northern Europe, Russia and the Middle East, and the exploration of the Atlantic and the discovery of Iceland, Greenland, and even America, are legendary. The Vikings are noted for their skilled craftsmanship in producing fine weapons and tools, intricate jewellery and a wide range of household equipment.

After the first devastating Viking raid on the monastery of Lindisfarne in 793, England became a rich source of income for the Vikings, and much sought after for colonisation. Most tangible evidence of Viking activity is in the north. York became a Viking capital, and excavations in Coppergate have revealed many intimate details of Viking life there. Northern England is rich in Viking sculpture, and densely covered with place-names of Viking origin (1).

The Vikings made steady progress westwards during the century after the attack on Lindisfarne. In 878, King Alfred defeated the Danish King Guthrum at the battle of Edington near the Bristol channel, and it was this decisive battle which halted the Danes and resulted in the formation of the Danelaw. The Treaty of Wedmore, drawn up after the battle, divided England in two, with the area to the north and east of a line from London to Chester coming under Danish rule. Though it was not a completely sepa-

1

rate entity in legal terms, the Danelaw represents the geographical extent of the main focus of Viking influence during this period. Within it were the Five Boroughs, established in the 880s as fortified centres: Nottingham, Derby, Leicester, Stamford and Lincoln. Many other towns and rural areas in the Danelaw were affected by the presence of the Vikings, as shown by documents, by archaeological evidence, by major and minor place-names. Language and legal terms still in use, personal names and the names of streets, all testify to the deep and enduring influence of the Vikings on the culture of the British Isles.

The FIRST VIKINGS in EAST ANGLIA
and the STORY of KING EDMUND

The Vikings first came to East Anglia in 866 AD. The Anglo-Saxon Chronicle, the account of English history written by monks in the reign of King Alfred (877-899), records this event in a brief and unemotional way:

> And the same year a great heathen army came into England and took up winter quarters in East Anglia; and there they were supplied with horses and the East Angles made peace with them.

Once they had established a base in East Anglia and stocked up with horses, the Vikings made successful attacks on York. Three years later, led by Ingvar and Ubbe, they returned to East Anglia, but this time met with opposition from Edmund, king of East Anglia. After a battle, they killed the king. The Anglo-Saxon Chronicle again summarises these momentous events in a very dry tone:

> In this year, the raiding army went across Mercia into East Anglia, and took up winter-quarters in Thetford; and that winter King Edmund fought against them, and the Danes had the victory, and killed the king and conquered all the land.

The story of the death of King Edmund was later written by the chronicler known as Abbo of Fleury, who was a monk, and wrote about a century later at Ramsey Abbey. Abbo dedicated his account to Dunstan, Archbishop of Canterbury. As a young man in the service of King Athelstan, Dunstan had heard the story of King Edmund's death from an old man. The old man, when in his turn a young man, had been King Edmund's sword-bearer, and hence an eye-witness.

According to Abbo, King Edmund was tied to a tree by the Danes, and lashed with whips. Despite his agonies, he continued to call on Christ. He was then pierced with arrows like Saint Sebastian, as if the Danes were at target practice, until, in Abbo's graphic words, he looked like a prickly hedgehog. Finally, he was beheaded. The king's head was taken by the Danes into the wood known as Haglesdun, and hidden in brambles. The survivors searched for the head so that they could bury the body and head together. By a miracle, the head responded to their calls, replying 'Hic, hic' ('here, here' in Latin), and they found it cradled in the paws of a huge wolf, which was guarding it. They buried the head and body of the king and constructed a small chapel there. After 28 years, miraculous events began to occur, and the king became known as a saint, and his remains were taken for re-burial at Bedricesgueord, now known as Bury St Edmunds. By a miracle, his body was found to be whole when translated, or moved, and there were no signs of scars. His grave was the scene of much devotion.

Where in fact was Edmund killed? Over the centuries, many places have been suggested, Hellesdon near Norwich, and Hoxne in Suffolk in particular. Apart from the name itself, Hellesdon near Norwich does not tie in with other aspects of the story. Hoxne is first mentioned in connection with King Edmund's death in the foundation charter of the abbey at Bury St Edmunds granted to the monks of Norwich by Bishop Herbert of Losinga in 1101. In later manuscripts, probably based on this account, Hoxne was again associated with Edmund's martyrdom. However, an earlier reference seems to pin-

point more precisely the place of martyrdom. Herman of Bury writing in about 1095 declared that the martyr was first buried at Sutton, close to the scene of his martyrdom, and that miraculous events occurred there after 28 years.

Recent research has discovered a 'Sutton' near a 'Haegelisdun'. Six miles south of Bury St Edmunds, there is an old field name Hellesden, close to a Sutton Hall. Two miles to the north are Kingshall Farm, Kingshall Street and Kingshall Green. These place-names also tie in with Abbo's account, as he implies that there was a royal estate and residence close to the site of Edmund's death. The fact that these names occur so close together (Hellesden being the wood where the Danes hid the king's head, and Sutton the place where the English buried him first and built a small chapel), and so close to Bury St Edmunds, is surely more than coincidence.

About 25 years after his death, a remarkable issue of coinage, known as the St Edmund memorial coinage, was minted and circulated in the eastern Danelaw under its Danish rulers. Around 2000 coins are known, all bearing on the obverse a central A, with the legend: SCE EADMUND REX within two circles; the reverse bears a central cross surrounded by an inscription, usually the name of the moneyer who struck the coins (2). These coins were used by the mixed Danish and Saxon population until about 920.

The coinage shows not only that Edmund was honoured as a saint within 25 years of his death, but also that the cult of the new saint was approved by the Danish successors of his murderers. The reasons for this apparent U-turn, in which Vikings newly converted to Christianity recognised their victim as a saint, must have been largely political, as indeed was their initial rapid conversion. What better way to make sure of their position and over-ride any potential opposition than by adopting the saint of the East Angles as their own?

The story of St Edmund, the East Anglian martyr, is one that conjures up persistent images of the barbaric Vikings. Yet the subsequent events show a far more complex relationship between the invaders and the local population than the stereotyped images suggest.

Fig 2. St. Edmund memorial coinage
PHOTO BY DAVID WICKS

SETTLEMENT

As a result of the Treaty of Wedmore in 878, Alfred gave Guthrum East Anglia. The entry in the Anglo-Saxon Chronicle for 879 reads: Guthrum and his army 'went from Cirencester into East Anglia, and settled there and shared out the land'. His kingdom comprised Norfolk, Suffolk, Essex, and parts of the South and East Midlands. Guthrum was then baptised, with King Alfred as his godfather, and he took the name of Athelstan. It was the custom for new Viking converts to take new Christian names. He issued coins in the name of Athelstan, based on the coinage of Alfred. This is a measure of how far he adopted Anglo-Saxon traditions, as Vikings in their homelands did not issue coins at this point, but used precious metals melted into ingots or chopped up (hack-silver) for exchange by weight. He died in 890.

Very few archaeological traces of the Vikings survive in Norfolk. No buildings or workshops, settlements or sites have been excavated which show where and how the Vikings lived after the land was shared out. However, there are many clues about the Vikings. Recent fieldwork and metal-detecting have brought to light Viking objects from all over Norfolk (3). The objects and the way they are decorated reveal that some were made in the Vikings' homelands in Scandinavia, and were brought to Norfolk with the settlers, and that others were made in Norfolk, still using Viking styles of decoration. The objects, jewellery and household equipment, weapons and horse-trappings, give us glimpses into the Vikings' everyday life in their new lands.

The settlers who followed Guthrum into East Anglia were on the whole poor farmers and their wives, whose jewellery was quite ordinary and mass-produced, made of copper alloy rather than of precious metals. Many of the objects are also very worn, presumably because the settlers, unable to afford new brooches and belt-fittings, wore their jewellery for a long time.

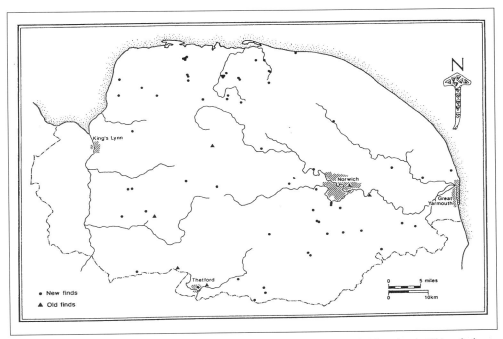

Fig 3. Map of early Viking findspots
MAP BY PHILLIP JUDGE

The settlers' poverty is confirmed also by the evidence of the place-names in Norfolk, where studies of the personal names involved have shown the settlers to be ordinary peasant farmers. The place-names give vital clues as to where the Vikings settled in Norfolk, because they gave new names to some existing villages and elsewhere created completely new villages and settlements with new names. Existing villages were given a Scandinavian personal name linked to the ending ton, the Old English word meaning village. Such a name is Grimston (Grim is a well known Scandinavian name). They also created new villages with names where both elements were Scandinavian, such as Ormesby, Orm being a Scandinavian man's name, and by meaning settlement in the Scandinavian languages. These names were given as big estates were divided up amongst the settlers. In the Flegg area around Great Yarmouth there are many such names: Ashby, Billockby, Clippesby, Filby, Hemsby, Herringby, Mautby, Oby, Ormesby, Rollesby, Scratby, Thrigby. Flegg itself is a Scandinavian word meaning reeds (4).

The Vikings also named natural features in their own language, such as reeds, streams, grass and ditches, and also man-made paths and roads, quays and fields. Occasionally these names are glimpsed in old maps where field-names retain these Scandinavian words. One area where a whole cluster of these names has been discovered is in north-west Norfolk in the Flitcham area. On a modern map, there is no trace of Viking place-names. But the old field-names contain Scandinavian words such as bekkr (stream), bryggja (jetty, quay), dik (ditch), gata (way, path, road), haugr (hill, mound), hvine (grass), kirkja (church), kraka (crow, raven), mikill (large), sik (ditch), stigr (path), toft (building site), thorp (secondary settlement), vangr (field). These field-names show that Vikings settled and farmed here. This picture could well be repeated elsewhere in Norfolk.

Peace followed the sharing out of land. The Five Boroughs of Leicester, Nottingham, Derby, Lincoln and Stamford, established in the 880s as fortified centres in the Danelaw, ensured stability in the Vikings' new terri-

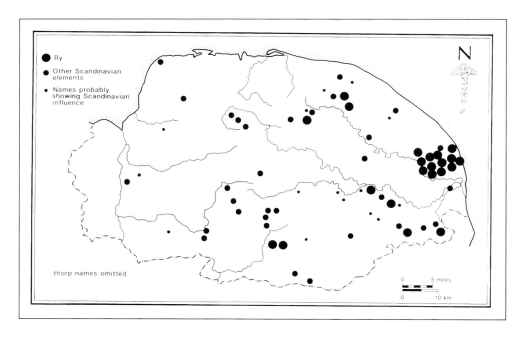

Fig 4. Map of place-names near Great Yarmouth
MAP BY PHILLIP JUDGE

tories. Between 879 and 918 when the Danelaw was reconquered by King Edward the Elder, king of the English, a whole generation of Danish farmers and their families lived and farmed peacefully in the north and east of England (5).

The security of the East Anglian kingdom under its Viking rulers was evidently such that it was used as a base for many raids to the west and the north. Not only that but they considered it safe enough to leave women and possessions there. Under the year 893, the Chronicle records that the Vikings, known as the Great Army, had many battles in the west country, and were eventually defeated and retired to their fortress in Essex, to re-assemble:

> *The survivors collected again before winter a large army from the East Angles and Northumbrians, placed their women and ships in safety in East Anglia, and went continuously by day and night until they reached a deserted city in the Wirral which is called Chester.*

The Danelaw came back under the control of King Edward the Elder in 917/918 but this did not lead to an expulsion of Danes - far from it. In fact the Chronicle records that Edward used both Danes and English to man the fortifications at Nottingham in 918, and we hear that both Danes and

English submitted to him and swore to keep the peace. There was by then a clearly well-established Anglo-Danish society in the Danelaw.

Fig 5. The Five Boroughs and the Danelaw after 879AD
MAP BY TREVOR ASHWIN

METALWORK *and* JEWELLERY
of the FIRST SETTLERS

The word Viking conjures up a ruthless warrior with fierce weapons. The portrayal of Vikings wielding swords and battle-axes on a stone-carving from Lindisfarne (6) captures the very spirit of contemporary reaction to the bands of invading warriors in the 8th century. Many weapons have been found in Viking graves and as stray finds throughout the Viking colonies, and documentary accounts show the terror the Vikings created. The great scholar Alcuin heard of the attack on Lindisfarne at the court of Charlemagne, and wrote to King Aethelred of Northumbria:

> *Lo, it is nearly 350 years that we and*
> *our fathers have inhabited this most*
> *lovely land, and never before has such terror*
> *appeared in Britain as we have now suffered*
> *from a pagan race, nor was it thought that such*
> *an inroad from the sea could be made.*

Many must have echoed his horror and distress.

In Norfolk, a number of Viking weapons have been discovered. Swords were the most prized of all weapons, and heroic stories were told by Vikings of the forging of swords, and of their supernatural powers. A 9th-century sword was found in the River Wensum in Norwich (7). Its findspot in the river is not likely to have been mere accident, but a deliberate custom. The sword was so strongly identified with a warrior - it was almost invested with a personality - that when he died, his sword was often bent to ' kill' it, and then flung into the river. Axes are also the typical Viking weapon; a bearded axe from the River Yare is a characteristic Scandinavian type. Horse equipment too testifies to the Vikings' warlike presence; stirrups are thought to have been introduced by the Vikings, as so many have been found in the Danelaw. Many Danish graves contain stirrups and other rich horse equipment. The iron was often decorated with copper alloy inlay in the form of spirals, as on the stirrup from Kilverstone.

But weapons and warlike activities do not tell the whole story. Most of the new finds are dress-fittings and jewellery, many of which would have been worn by women, otherwise only briefly glimpsed in the historical records. We know from the Anglo-Saxon Chronicle that the Great Army was accompanied by women in the 890s, as mentioned already. They must have been here before that, however. Once Guthrum had shared out the land in 879, women would certainly have come over to join the first settlers. The settlers may also have inter-married with the local population.

Fig 7. Sword from the River Wensum at Norwich, 9th Century
COPYRIGHT BRITISH MUSEUM

Fig 6. Lindisfarne stone showing possible Vikings with raised swords
COPYRIGHT ENGLISH HERITAGE PHOTO LIBRARY

The FIRST SETTLERS

One of the first Vikings to travel to Norfolk in the 860s must have dropped a treasured possession on the banks of the River Wensum at Bylaugh, near North Elmham (8).

It is a small gilded copper alloy mount, once used to decorate a box. It shows a horseman being greeted by a woman with a shield, with the end of her trailing dress broken off. This scene can be interpreted as a valkyrie, in pagan belief one of Odin's followers, welcoming a Viking warrior to Valhall, Odin's kingdom. This pagan scene was obviously very popular in the Viking world, as it was also carved on sculpture in the north of England (as at Sockburn on Tees), and on picture stones of the late 8th, early 9th centuries on Gotland in the Baltic. Bronze and silver pendants in the form of female figures with drinking-horns also occur in the late 9th century, particularly in Sweden. A horse and rider brooch (perhaps an echo of the same tradition) from Fulmodestone, Norfolk (12), must also have been worn by an early settler.

Fig 8. Mount from Bylaugh, showing Valkyrie welcoming horseman to Valhall
PHOTO BY DAVID WICKS

*Fig 10. Copper alloy mount
from Norwich*
PHOTO BY DAVID WICKS

Fig 9. Copper alloy harness mount
PHOTO BY DAVID WICKS

Fig 11. Iron stirrup with copper alloy plating, from Kilverstone
PHOTO BY DAVID WICKS

13

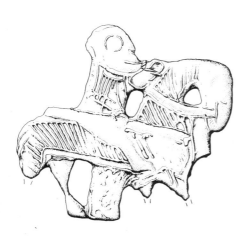

Fig 12. Horse and rider brooch from Fulmodestone
DRAWING BY SUSAN WHITE

Fig 13. Thor's hammer from South Lopham
PHOTO BY DAVID WICKS

Three other East Anglian stray finds also reflect pagan belief, a silver Thor's hammer found at Sibton, Suffolk, another made of silver from Surlingham, Norfolk and another, made of gold alloy, found at South Lopham (14). The hammer was the symbol of the god Thor, the powerful god of Norse mythology who was popular among the peasant farmers. Miniature versions were worn as pendants to protect the wearer from mishap. Thor's hammers are found in graves and hoards in the north of England, as in the vast hoard of silver found on the banks of the River Ribble at Cuerdale in Lancashire.

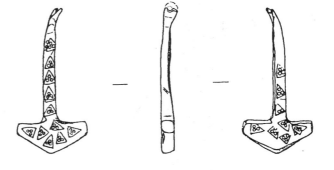

Fig 14. Thor's hammer from South Lopham
DRAWING BY ANNE HOLNESS
NORWICH CASTLE MUSEUM

14

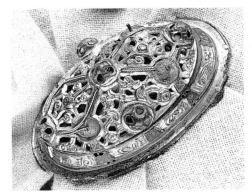

Fig 15. *One of a pair of oval brooches from Santon Downham*
PHOTO BY DAVID WICKS

Of the first settlers themselves, the only evidence is their burials. Pagan burials can be identified because people were buried with all their possessions for use in the afterlife. Only the first generation of settlers were pagan - they were converted rapidly to Christianity. Christians were not buried with their belongings because they believed in a spiritual, not a physical, afterlife. Probably in the late 9th century, a Viking man and woman were buried according to pagan custom in a double grave at Santon Downham, now Lynford parish (15). The burial was discovered in 1867. Nothing survives in the grave except the metalwork, but this can give us clues about what the couple might have worn, and their most favoured possessions. The woman was buried with a pair of oval brooches, the man with a sword. Oval brooches were used to fasten the shoulders of an overdress (16) and were a common part of women's dress from the 9th to the mid 10th centuries. They range from elaborate double-shelled ones with openwork outer shells often further decorated with silver wire (as here) to cast, rather crudely decorated single-shelled brooches.

Fig 16. *Viking man and woman*
COPYRIGHT THE ANGLO-DANISH
VIKING PROJECT

Until recently, the only other pagan burial in East Anglia was that of a well-to-do woman discovered at Saffron Walden in Essex in 1876. The skeleton had a necklace composed of two silver pendants, two carnelian, two glass and two crystal beads (17).

The burial of a man was excavated at Harling in 1986 , and although it was nothing like as rich as the other two, it was a pagan burial of late 9th or early 10th-century date. The skeleton was found with knives, including one with a pivoting blade, a whetstone to sharpen the knife, a spur and a toilet implement (18).

The other essential piece of jewellery for a Viking woman of the late 9th, early 10th century was the trefoil brooch, as common as oval brooches and in fashion at roughly the same time. They were used to hold a shawl in place, and in the Scandinavian homelands, they were worn with a pair of oval brooches. The fashion in the Viking colonies in England seems to have developed differently, and the trefoil brooch took over from the oval brooches. The trefoil brooch was based on trefoil harness mounts with beautiful leaf decoration, which Vikings picked up in Germany and took back to Scandinavia and later altered into brooches. These became

16

Fig 17. Pendants and necklace from Saffron Walden
COPYRIGHT SAFFRON
WALDEN MUSEUM

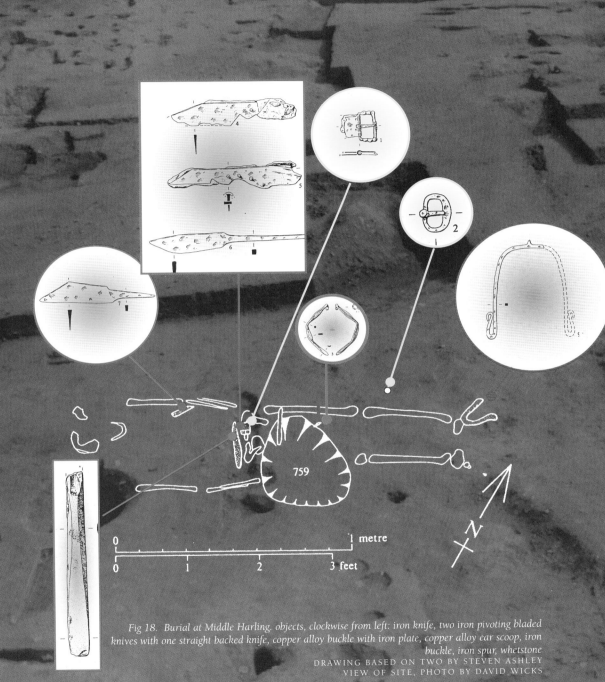

Fig 18. Burial at Middle Harling, objects, clockwise from left: iron knife, two iron pivoting bladed knives with one straight backed knife, copper alloy buckle with iron plate, copper alloy ear scoop, iron buckle, iron spur, whetstone

DRAWING BASED ON TWO BY STEVEN ASHLEY
VIEW OF SITE, PHOTO BY DAVID WICKS

so popular that brooches based on this design were made all over Scandinavia, from expensive and elaborate gold and silver examples at one end of the scale, to more ordinary ones of copper alloy.

Pewter trefoil brooches were mass-produced in antler moulds (such as those found at Hedeby, the great Viking trading centre in southern Denmark, now in north Germany). The antler moulds could be used over and over again, so many identical brooches could be made. Some have very stylised leaf decoration but others have animal ornament so

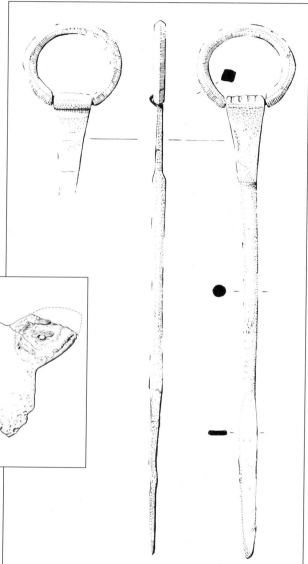

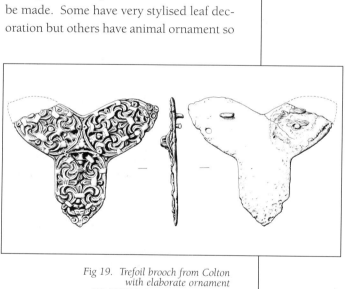

Fig 19. Trefoil brooch from Colton with elaborate ornament
DRAWING BY SUSAN WHITE

much loved by the Vikings. Many trefoil brooches (some only fragments) have been found in Norfolk and Suffolk, and most have very stylised leaf decoration. Only two, the arm of a brooch from Taverham and a complete brooch from Colton (19) have very

Fig 20. Ringed pin from Brooke
DRAWING BY KENNETH PENN

fine, cast leaf decoration, close to the decoration of the originals copied by the Vikings. One brooch, from Carlton Colville, has a loop on the reverse, as well as the usual lug and catchplate to pin the brooch in place. The loop was meant for a pendant, and this is a clue that it was made in Scandinavia. Others were probably made in Norfolk.

At the same date, a Viking man might wear a ringed dress pin to fasten his cloak. Such a pin was found at Brooke in 1991 (20), and a similar pin without its ring was discovered at Congham. The ringed pin originated in the eastern Baltic, and many examples have been excavated in Hedeby and Birka (the large Viking town on the east coast of Sweden, north of Stockholm). The pin may have been worn by a Viking who came to Norfolk from Hedeby. These pins were held in place by a thong or cord tied to the ring and then to the end of the pin once it had been pushed through the cloth.

SETTLING DOWN,

the 10*th* CENTURY

Other favourite and more ordinary brooches worn by the early settlers have been found across Norfolk. Many were made in Scandinavia. One type is a lozenge-shaped brooch with a moulded animal head like a cat at each corner (21). Several examples have been recovered from East Anglia, all copper alloy and some very worn which suggests they were in use for a long time. These brooches were cast in a mould, such as one found at Hedeby. This brooch type has been found right across the Viking world from Russia to Dublin: what clearer evidence could there be of Viking exploration and expansion?

Small domed disc brooches, again cast in moulds, were another popular fashion. Seven recent finds are decorated with three cat-like animal-heads seen from above, with large staring eyes. They face inwards, and are separated from each other by the lobes of a trefoil. These beady-eyed animals are absolutely classic examples of a Viking style

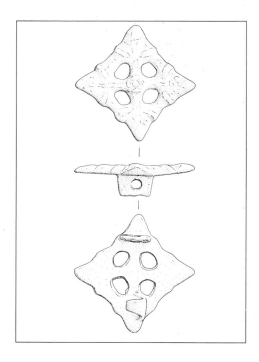

Fig 21. Lozenge-shaped brooch from Stoke Holy Cross
DRAWING BY STEVEN ASHLEY

of ornament called the Borre style after a place in Norway on Oslo fjord where decorated metalwork was found. Again the type is widespread in the Viking homelands, with an especially large concentration in Birka. The brooch from Heckingham (22) is the finest example, with intact double lug and catch-plate on the reverse, and a loop for a pendant, a sure sign of Scandinavian origin. Two

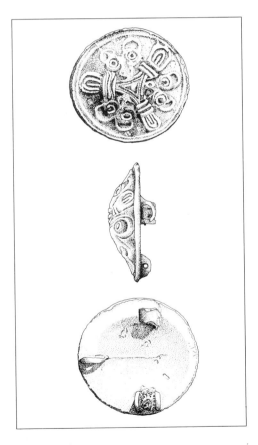

brooches, one from West Caister and one from Keswick, are of a slightly different but related type, with three animal heads facing outwards, and a complex pattern of interlacing, billeted bands. Brooches of this type have been found at Birka in Sweden, Hedeby and Trelleborg in Denmark, and in the Faroes.

Besides these cat-like animals, the Borre style has animals known as gripping beasts, which grip anything in sight, and an interlace motif known as a ring-knot. The ring-knot consists of double loops, often sprouting from a lozenge or a triangle. These other elements of the Borre style are best seen on the silver pendants from the Saffron Walden burial (17).

The best example of the Borre style from Norfolk is on a large strap-end from Walsingham (23). Strap-ends, attached to the end of belts, were very popular at this period, and decorated the belt as well as keeping it from fraying or curling. The strap-end from Walsingham is decorated with a 'ring-chain' motif, in which the double loops of the Borre ring-knot are repeated to form a chain pattern. This same 'ring-chain' motif decorates a fragment of a strap-end from Blo Norton (24). A buckle from Sculthorpe has a Borre-style cat-like animal in the centre, its paws gripping the ends of the pin bar (25). A superb animal-head found at North Creake has ring-chain interlace around its ears and eyes, with a triangle between two loops (26). The pierced hole through the end of the animal's neck suggests it was attached to a chain.

Fig 22. Convex disc brooch from Heckingham with three cat-like animals, Borre Style
DRAWING BY DAVID FOX

21

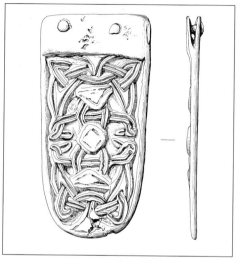

Fig 23. *Borre-style strap-end*
from Walsingham
DRAWING BY SUE WHITE

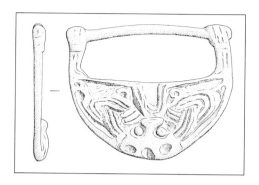

Fig 25. *Borre-style buckle from Sculthorpe*
DRAWING BY STEVEN ASHLEY

Fig 24. *Borre-style strap-end*
from Blo Norton
PHOTO BY DAVID WICKS

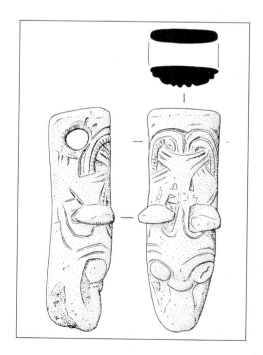

Fig 26. *Borre-style animal-head terminal*
from North Creake
DRAWING BY STEVEN ASHLEY

Vikings also played games in their spare time, and a gaming-piece from Bawdsey, Suffolk, (27) gives us a rare glimpse of Viking leisure pursuits. It is made of jet, probably from Whitby which was the best source of jet at this date, and it is decorated with the Borre ring-chain motif, and ring-and-dot. It may have been used for the Viking game known as hnefatafl in which one group of pieces tries to take the king belonging to the other side.

Once the Vikings settled, they began adopting some of the local fashions and the domed disc brooch was overtaken by a flat disc brooch, which was a Saxon tradition of the 9th century. Flat brooches decorated with a knotted interlace pattern became very popular, especially in East Anglia. The interlace springs from the arms of a lozenge, with a sunken circle in the centre. This interlace pattern is a distant relative of the Viking Borre style. The large number found in Norfolk suggests that they may have been made in the county, perhaps in or around Norwich. Many of the brooches are extremely worn, which suggests they too were in use for a very long period, just like the imported brooches. Often the decoration is quite crudely done, but occasionally, there is a more elaborate brooch, such as one excavated from the Castle Bailey site in Norwich (28). On this brooch the craftsman had coated the border of engraved diagonal lines with white metal to make a decorative contrast with the copper alloy.

Fig 27. Borre-style gaming-piece from Bawdsey, Suffolk
COPYRIGHT IPSWICH BOROUGH
COUNCIL MUSEUMS & GALLERIES

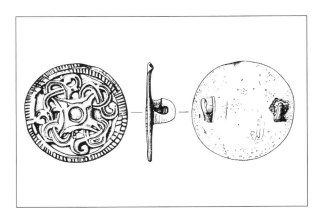

Fig 28. Anglian flat disc brooch from Norwich Castle Bailey
DRAWING BY RYSZARD HAJDUL,
COPYRIGHT NORFOLK ARCHAEOLOGY UNIT

23

LATER 10th CENTURY

A bit later in the 10th century, domed disc brooches with a different sort of animal decoration were brought in to East Anglia by a new wave of settlers, presumably coming to join their relatives. The Jellinge style, named after objects found in the royal burial at Jelling, Jutland, overlaps with the Borre style. Six domed brooches decorated in this style have been discovered in Norfolk. The typical animal is ribbon-like, in an s-shape, and has a rounded head (29).

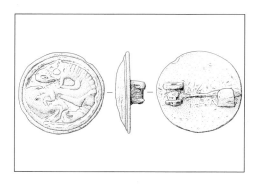

Fig 29. Convex disc brooch with Jellinge-style animal ornament
DRAWING BY STEVEN ASHLEY

The Vikings became Christian very soon after they settled in Norfolk. In Yorkshire, the newly-converted Vikings quickly adopted the Christian custom of marking graves with stone crosses. As Norfolk's native stone is flint, which is unsuitable for stone monuments, the Vikings in Norfolk could not adopt this Christian custom quite so readily. However, they imported limestone from the Midlands, and one fragment of a cross-shaft decorated with Viking ornament survives. This is known as the St Vedast cross. It is so named because it was found in the wall of a house which was built on the site of the church of St Vedast and St Amant (demolished in 1540), in Rose Lane, Norwich. The house, demolished for road-widening in 1896, incorporated part of the churchyard wall into which the stone had been built.

Only two faces of the shaft are decorated. Packed into an arched frame on the main face are two animals, and another pair of animals are similarly crowded into the side panel (30). The animal ornament is 'Mammen' style, named after grave-finds of the mid-10th century from Mammen in Denmark.

Fig 30. Stone carving of Mammen style, now in the Keep of Norwich Castle Museum
DRAWING BY KAREN GUFFOG
COPYRIGHT
ENGLISH HERITAGE PHOTO LIBRARY

0   5   10   15   20   25 cms

The DEVELOPMENT of
THETFORD & NORWICH

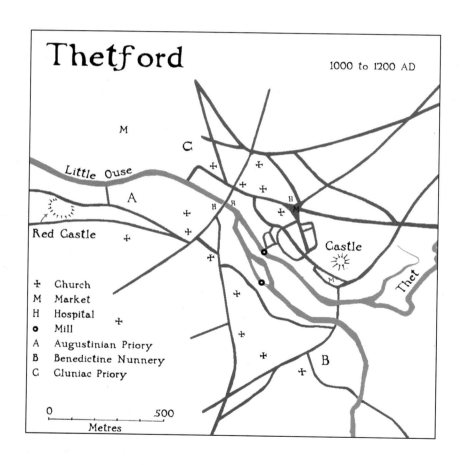

Fig 31. Map of Thetford
DRAWING BY HOSTE SPALDING

The references to Thetford and Norwich in the Anglo-Saxon Chronicle are clear - if brief - evidence of Viking activity in both towns. Their development as towns may in fact be due to the presence of the Vikings and archaeology provides some clues about this.

The location of Thetford at a junction of N/S, E/W routes was of course a vital factor in its development, and it is no doubt because of this that the Vikings wintered there in 869. Once they settled there, they must have created a new burst of economic growth, and the pottery industry probably resulted from changes caused by Danish settlement. The town certainly flourished in the 10th century, as excavations have shown, with extensive evidence of crafts and industries, as well as the renowned pottery industry. Thetford-ware has a wide distribution in the Danelaw, and similar pottery was produced in a number of sites in East Anglia.

Norwich superseded landlocked Thetford in importance from the 11th century largely because of its easier access to the sea. Danish settlement in the area from the 9th century onwards could well have provided the impetus for the development of Norwich, the crucial period of its emergence being from 850 to 925. The fortified 'burh' was probably located in the Magdalen Street area; its D-shaped enclosure has been traced in the street-pattern there. Many street names confirm the Scandinavian influence in Norwich:

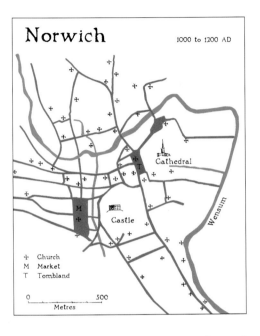

Fig 32. Map of Norwich
DRAWING BY HOSTE SPALDING

the ending 'gate' comes from Old Norse gata or street. Finkelgate has two Scandinavian elements, finkel meaning 'crooked', or, as suggested recently 'cuddle', the street name thus being translated 'Lovers' Lane'. Other street names, now lost, also have Scandinavian elements, such as those on the Ber Street escarpment: Holgate, meaning street in the hollow (now Mariners Lane); and Skygate, or skeidgata, meaning 'way on the ridge' (now Horns Lane). Churches dedicated to Scandinavian saints, two to St Olave in King Street (itself a Danish name, from konungr, king), and two to St Clement in Colegate and Conesford also reflect the

27

Scandinavian presence, though probably 11th century dedications.

The jewellery reflects these mixed cultures flourishing in Norwich in the 10th and 11th centuries. The flat disc brooches so beloved of the Saxons, now decorated with Scandinavian ornament, are a sure sign of mixed traditions and fashions.

The Danes in Norfolk may well have been responsible for transforming the economy of the region, for stimulating the emergence of Thetford and Norwich as substantial towns, and for the appearance of Thetford-ware pottery. This would tie in with what is known of Viking activity in other areas, especially York and Lincoln, where pottery was among the industries they established. They were certainly shrewd business men, and quick to pick up new ideas, and the trading-centres they founded in their colonies succeeded for the very reason that they were ready to innovate, introducing new industries not known in their homelands, such as pottery, and to follow the Saxon tradition of issuing coinage, rather than using silver by weight.

Fig 33. Iron stirrup (fig.11), iron axe head from River Yare, Surlingham Ferry. On axe head: strap end, mount from Bylaugh (fig.8), strap end from Blo Norton (fig.24). Clockwise from top left: bridle cheekpiece (fig.40), bridle cheekpiece (fig .39), bird brooch (fig.35), buckle (fig.25), animal-head terminal (fig.26), disc brooch (fig.28), ringed pin (fig.20), mount (fig.10)

NEW VIKING RAIDS

in the LATE 10*th* CENTURY

In the late 10th century, after a long period of peace, Viking raids began again. This time the raids were not about colonisation by farmers and merchants but about the need for wealth as the eastern trade-routes had dried up. The Scandinavian countries were becoming more powerful as integrated kingdoms at this period, especially Denmark under King Harald Bluetooth, who consolidated his power with fortresses, causeways and bridges to unite his far-flung country. From now until the first decade of the 11th century, the English paid huge Danegelds to the Vikings to prevent further attacks - the biggest payment recorded was in 1011, when the Danegeld was a massive £48000.

One of the first of these new raids culminated in the over-running of Ipswich in 991, just before the famous battle of Maldon, won by the Vikings and commemorated in the Anglo-Saxon poem *The Battle of Maldon*. These raids were of course directed at a well- .

established Anglo-Danish population, and the raiders this time were probably of mixed nationality, as both King Olaf Tryggvason of Norway and Svein Forkbeard of Denmark were the masterminds behind them.

In 1004, Thetford and Norwich were ravaged and burnt. The Anglo-Saxon Chronicle captures well the complexity of the situation. The ealdorman of East Anglia was Ulfcetel, obviously a Dane:

> *In this year Swein came with his fleet to Norwich and completely ravaged and burnt the borough. Then Ulfcetel with the councillors in East Anglia determined that it would be better to buy peace from the army before they did too much damage in the country, for they had come unexpectedly and he had not much time to collect his army. Then, under cover of the truce which was supposed to lie between them, the Danish army stole inland from the ships, and directed their course to Thetford.*

29

When Ulfcetel perceived that, he sent orders that the ships were to be hewn to bits, but those for whom he intended this failed him; he then collected his army secretly, as quickly as he could. And the Danish army then came to Thetford within three weeks after their ravaging of Norwich, and remained inside there one night, and ravaged and burnt the borough. Then in the morning, when they wished to go to their ships, Ulfcetel arrived with his troops to offer battle there. And they resolutely joined battle, and many fell slain on both sides. There the flower of the East Anglian people was killed. But if their full strength had been there, the Danes would never have got back to their ships; as they themselves said they never met worse fighting in England than Ulfcetel dealt to them.

These raids were the prelude to Svein's invasion of England in AD 1013. His son Cnut became king of England on his death in 1016, ruling Denmark, Norway and 'part of the Swedes too'.

The poem Cnutsdrapa praises King Cnut's brave deeds, among them a raid on Norwich in 1016, one of the last Viking raids:

> *Gracious giver of mighty gifts you made corslets red in Norwich you will lose your life before your courage fails.*

This is a very Viking sort of poem, yet Cnut was quite a different character of king. From then on there was peace, and a true fusion of English and Scandinavian traditions under Cnut's enlightened and cosmopolitan reign. His kingdom, based at Winchester, reached far beyond the bounds of the old Danelaw of the 9th/10th centuries. Cnut built a church dedicated to St Edmund at Ashingdon, Essex, on the site of his victory over Edmund Ironside, the son of Aethelred the Unready.

In addition, he rebuilt the church at Bury St Edmunds, and placed Edmund's shrine in the care of the Bendictine monks. He endowed the community with lavish gifts, and made a pilgrimage there in 1020. A Christian cosmopolitan king, and shrewd politician, he made amends for the deeds of his ancestors in this way in order to consolidate his power. In a sense, this was no more than earlier Vikings had done, when they were converted to Christianity for political reasons. But the scale of Cnut's empire, and the nature of his kingship, are a measure of how the Viking warrior had become the medieval ruler. Under Cnut's hands, the Viking world was transformed. Cnut died in 1035, and with his death, the Viking Age in England was really over, though Viking influence lingered on.

The 11*th* CENTURY

In the 11th century, the cultures of England and Scandinavia were linked so closely that Viking art styles were influenced by English art, as well as the other way round. The Ringerike and the Urnes styles, named after places in Norway, were happily adopted throughout the British Isles, and developed along their own lines, reflecting the fusion of the two cultures from court level down through society. Quite ordinary artifacts decorated with both these styles have been found in Norfolk. Most are casual losses and were the possessions of farmers and their families, many of mixed race.

The Ringerike style, named after stone carvings in the Ringerike area north of Oslo, has characteristically lively animals with tendrils sprouting wildly from their heads and necks and tails. It was influenced by the Saxon Winchester style, which had acanthus leaves and tendrils forming elaborate decoration on manuscripts, metalwork and sculpture. This style developed around the royal court

at Winchester in the late 10th century.

The classic example of the Ringerike style in England is on the St Paul's grave-stone now in the Museum of London (34). The leaf at the corner is a very distinctive motif, and the great beast in the centre has the sprouting tendrils so much the keynote of this style. The typical Ringerike tendrils appear in rather cruder form on many recent finds from East Anglia. The finds range from dress-fittings to harness pendants and horse equipment. Many of these are very standardised, with similar examples occurring in Norfolk, Suffolk and Lincolnshire, suggesting mass-production, with craftsmen using the same or similar moulds, and designs perhaps passing from one to another.

New types of dress-fittings were fashionable in the 11th century. A buckle from Thetford has a triangular frame, decorated with engraved stylised animal heads. Another

*Fig 34. Ringerike-style ornament on a
gravestone from St. Paul's, now Museum of London*
COPYRIGHT MUSEUM OF LONDON
PICTURE LIBRARY

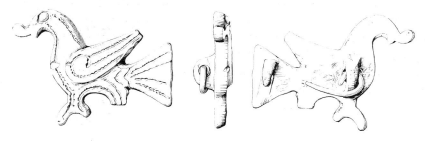

*Fig 35. Ringerike-style bird brooch
from Stoke Holy Cross*
DRAWING BY SUSAN WHITE

reflects the new Viking raids in the late 10th century. A fragment of a horse-harness pendant, perhaps from Norwich, is decorated with a leaf flanked by two animal heads, with tendrils on their muzzles (36).

Another much more common find is a group of triangular mounts (37), which often have traces of iron strips on the reverse, and iron rivets. At first they were thought to be book-mounts, but their sturdiness and the presence of iron fittings makes this unlikely. In addition, far too many of these mounts have been found to be associated with books; in this period, books were rare indeed. More recently, they were identified as box-mounts.

Fig 36. Ringerike-style harness-mount from Norwich
PHOTO BY DAVID WICKS

buckle from Grimston has engraved lines, and a projecting trefoil acted as a tongue-rest. Most striking of all is a brooch shaped like a bird, made of copper alloy, from Stoke Holy Cross (35). The craftsman engraved the details of spiral wings, fan-shaped tail, and tendril at the end of the beak. There is a lug and catchplate on the reverse, and a complete pin made of copper alloy wire. Similar bird brooches are known from Scandinavia, ranging from a lead one from Lund in Sweden, dated to between 1020-50, to a later and more elaborate silver openwork bird brooch, this time in the Urnes style from Gresli in Norway.

Most surviving 11th-century metalwork is part of horse-harness which presumably

Fig 37. Ringerike-style stirrup mount from Walsingham
PHOTO BY DAVID WICKS

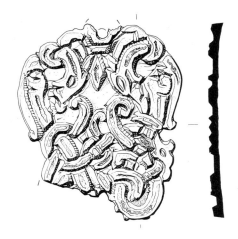

*Fig 38. Ringerike-style flat mount from
Middle Harling*
DRAWING BY STEVEN ASHLEY

An even more recent idea, found in David Williams's forthcoming book, is that they are stirrup mounts which are riveted to the stirrup leather, with the flange fitting under the edge of the stirrup loop. They have only three rivet holes for attachment, which is not very secure. Many of the recent finds have substantial traces of iron on the reverse, and one from Winchester has an iron strip on the reverse, parallel with the body of the mount. The iron strip could be an additional way of securing the mount to the stirrup leather. The widespread distribution of these mounts in rural and urban areas supports the idea that they were horse equipment, although they may have been used for more than one purpose.

*Fig 39. Ringerike-style cheekpiece from
St. Martin-at-Palace Plain, Norwich*
PHOTO BY DAVID WICKS

An elaborate mount excavated at Middle Harling may also have been a harness decoration (38). It is flat and of a slightly different form from the triangular mounts described above. It is decorated with a pair of animals, interlacing and intertwining with each other. There is a leaf between the animal heads, a typical Ringerike motif. The animal bodies are inlaid with zig-zag silver wire.

Bridle cheekpieces are perhaps the most common part of horse-harness to survive. Two bridle cheekpiece fragments are deco-

rated in the same style. Both show animal heads in profile. One, excavated at St Martin-at-Palace-Plain, Norwich (39), has rather crude animal head with tendrils forming the mane. The other from Stoke Holy Cross is of much finer workmanship (40). It is broken at the neck of the animal and has fine engraved tendrils and a mane of tendrils. The curve of the neck and the lively way the tendrils are engraved show this style at its best. On the basis of a complete cheekpiece from Angsby, Uppland in Sweden (Uppsala Museum UMF 4573) this animal head

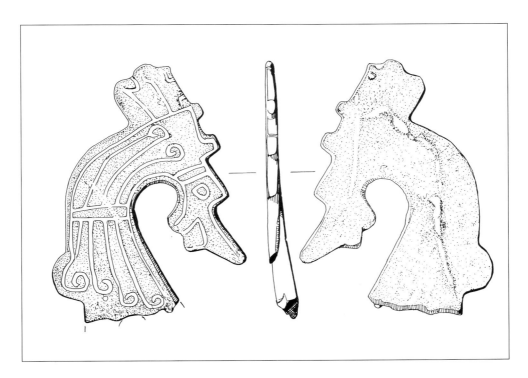

Fig 40. Ringerike-style cheekpiece from Stoke Holy Cross
DRAWING BY KENNETH PENN

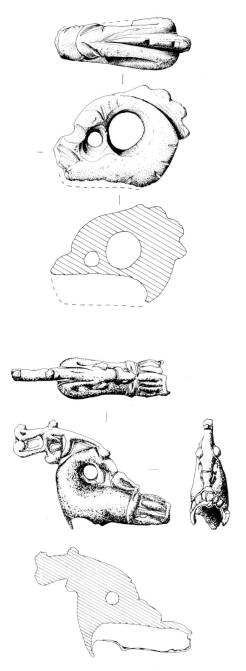

would have projected on one side of the cheekpiece with a corresponding head on the other side. Where the necks join, there is a pierced hole, through which the bridle bit would be secured. Above the pierced hole, is a bar with pierced terminal for the bridle harness.

The classic Ringerike style is also found on a group of three-dimensional animal-heads with manes formed of tendrils. Many have traces of solder inside, by which they would have been attached. (41) Some similar copper alloy animal-headed mounts have been identified recently by David Williams on an iron stirrup in the Ashmolean Museum, Oxford. These are attached with solder to the corners of the foot-rest and the shoulders just below the loop. Whether all the newly recorded examples come from stirrups is a matter of debate, and again, maybe

Fig 41. Ringerike-style stirrup finials
a) with crest from Swafield
b) with flying mare from Gooderstone
DRAWING A) BY SUSAN WHITE

they were used for more than one purpose.

The latest Viking art style was the Urnes style of the mid and late 11th century, named after the vigorous wood-carvings from the first stave church at Urnes, Norway, now built into the north wall of a younger stave church. Sinuous animals intertwine with thin ribbons and snakes, creating a lively and delicate pattern. The animals are carved almost in the round, and this is the impression given on the metalwork too, where the interlacing animals are usually

Fig 43 . Urnes-style mount
PHOTO BY DAVID WICKS

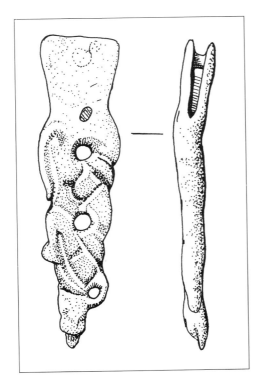

Fig 42. Urnes-style strap-end from Norwich
DRAWING BY KENNETH PENN

cast in openwork, and then finished off with a file, making a rounded surface. Dress-fittings decorated in this style are rare, however, and an exciting new find from Norwich is the first Urnes style strap-end from Norfolk - and possibly the first from the Danelaw (42). The strap-end is narrow, with the animal-head at the terminal much like the Saxon strap-ends of the 9th century. However, this animal head is tiny and elongated, typical of Urnes animals, and it has an interlacing openwork ribbon-like body which forms the body of the strap-end. There is a split end with two rivet holes to attach the strap in the usual way. Another new find is an openwork copper alloy

*Fig 44. Urnes-style stirrup mount
from Norwich*
PHOTO BY DAVID WICKS

brooch from Shotley in Suffolk in the form of a serpentine animal, intertwining with tendrils, a rather crude version of the splendid silver Urnes brooches.

Most of the other pieces of Urnes style metalwork are box or casket mounts or harness-fittings.

As with the earlier mounts, the design was standardised to a certain extent. Three mounts all have a sinuous interlacing animal curling into an intricate circle, with the head on a long projecting neck (43). There is a rivet through the muzzle of the animal, and another through its body. Triangular stirrup-mounts, slightly convex, of the type already described, are also decorated with the Urnes style. One from Norwich itself is a fine example, though the apex of the mount is missing (44).

The influence of the Vikings lived on long after the Norman Conquest. The latest flow-

ering of the Urnes style in Norfolk is in the
early 12th century: a capital from the early
cloisters of the cathedral (45). It is a perfect
piece of Romanesque sculpture, decorated
with pairs of animals with interlacing snakes
or ribbons, typical of Urnes intricacy. The
style of ornament had entered into the craftsman's repertoire.

Fig 45. Urnes-style cathedral capital,
early 12th Century

OTHER VIKING
PERIOD OBJECTS

Some rare precious objects have been discovered. A gold finger-ring from Thetford is made of a strip of gold with tapering ends twisted round each other. The wider part forming the bezel is decorated with punched annulets within a stepped-triangular frame. Silver ingots were found at Ditchingham, Hindringham and Hockwold-cum-Wilton. They are rare finds in England because the new settlers were quick to issue coins in the Anglo-Saxon manner, rather than using bullion for exchange as in the homelands. A number of spherical bronze weights, based on oriental weight systems, from Harling (46) and elsewhere in Norfolk reflect trading activities. Recent finds of dirhams, silver Arabic coins, such as one at Burnham, are also the result of Viking trading activity. Assemblages from sites such as Harling and Burnham give a clue about the sort of settlements with which the Vikings would have traded.

Many ordinary everyday objects go undetected, as they have little decoration to distinguish them from objects of Saxon manufacture. Simple bone pins, like those from Thetford, iron tools, pots and cooking vessels would be much the same in appearance whether they were Viking or Saxon. There are many ordinary, undecorated objects in the Viking homelands.

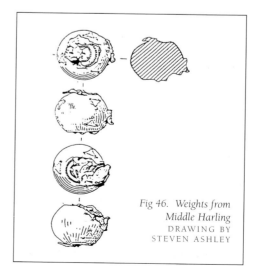

Fig 46. Weights from Middle Harling
DRAWING BY STEVEN ASHLEY

The VIKINGS
in NORFOLK

The Vikings have left clear signs of their presence throughout their colonies. Artistic achievement, place-names, legal terms, and language all survive to this day as lasting testimonies. The artifacts, the jewellery and the horse-equipment, the weapons and the objects relating to trade, are the only tangible legacy in East Anglia, a rich and ever-growing source of information about the nature of Viking settlement in the kingdom.

The earliest finds reflect the life of the new settlers, who kept to their pagan beliefs for perhaps only a generation. Once the Vikings settled, they became Christians rapidly. They presumably intermarried with Saxons, and even adopted some of the Saxon traditions of jewellery. However, they went on using their much loved styles of decoration, and every now and then, as relatives came over from the homelands to join them, new Scandinavian ornament became fashionable. The recent discoveries of everyday objects date from the 9th to the 11th centuries, from the period of the first settlement to the final

Anglo-Scandinavian period under King Cnut.

The finds are widespread in the county, which reflects a scattered pattern of rural settlement. This pattern is repeated in the Viking homelands of Denmark, as many recent discoveries there by metal-detector have revealed. The 'lowly' quality of much of the East Anglian metalwork reflects the relative poverty of the settlers, who were mostly ordinary peasant farmers and their wives. But this is not something unique to this region. Many of the new discoveries in Denmark are of similar quality, confirming that the settlers in East Anglia were of similar backgrounds. The incomers were seeking land like their own back home and once settled, they carried on their lives much as before.

41

FURTHER
READING

Biddle, Martin, ed.1990, *Object and Economy in Medieval Winchester*, Winchester Studies 7, ii

Campbell, J, 1975, *Norwich* (London)

Graham-Campbell, J, 1980, *Viking Artifacts* (London)

Hinton, David, 1990, *Archaeology, Economy and Society* (London)

Margeson, Sue, 1986, 'A Group of Late Saxon Mounts from Norfolk', *Norfolk Archaeology*, 323-327

Margeson, Sue, 1996 'Viking Settlement in Norfolk: a Study of New Evidence' in Margeson, S, Ayers, B, and Heywood, S, eds, *A Festival of Norfolk Archaeology*, (Norwich), 47-57

McCarthy, M, and Brook, C, 1988, *Medieval Pottery in Britain AD900-1600* (Leicester)

Robinson, P, 'Some Late Saxon Mounts from Wiltshire', *Wiltshire Archaeology and Natural History Magazine*, 85, 63-69

Rogerson, Andrew, and Dallas, Caroline, 1984, *Excavations in Thetford 1948-59 and 1973-77*, East Anglian Archaeology 22

Sandred, K, 1979, 'Scandinavian Place-Names and Appellatives in Norfolk, A Study of the Medieval Field-Name of Flitcham', *Namm och Bygd*, 67, 1-4, 98-122

Sandred, K, 1987, ' The Vikings in Norfolk, some observations on the place-names in -by', in *Proceedings of the Tenth Viking Congress* (Universitetes Oldsaksamlings Skrifter, Ny rekke nr. 9, Oslo)

Williams, D, forthcoming, *A Classification and Catalogue of Late Saxon Stirrup-Strap Mounts*, Council for British Archaeology Monograph Series

Williamson, T, 1993, *The Origins of Norfolk* (Manchester)

Wilson, D M, 1964, *Anglo-Saxon Ornamental Metalwork, 700-1100, in the British Museum* (London)